I0759601

A Caregiver's COMPANION

Scriptures, Hymns, and Forty Years of Insights for Life's Toughest Role

PETER W. ROSENBERGER

FIDELIS PUBLISHING ®

ISBN: 9798992418606
ISBN (eBook): 9798992418613

A Caregiver's Companion:
Daily Inspiration for Life's Toughest Role

Cover and Interior Design by Diana Lawrence
Edited by Amanda Varian

Order at www.faithfultext.com for a significant discount. Email info@fidelispublishing.com to inquire about bulk purchase discounts.

Fidelis Publishing, LLC • Winchester, VA / Nashville, TN • fidelispublishing.com

Manufactured in the United States of America

10 9 8 7 6 5 4 3 2 1

For my inlaws:

James A. Parker

Andrea Parker Killingsworth

and Bobby Killingsworth

And in memory of

Carol L. Parker

Thank you for Gracie–

and for grace.

Introduction

For years, as a caregiver, I often found myself drowning in well-meaning but empty platitudes, sincere but misguided theology—or the harder wound: not silence itself, but the absence of presence from those who didn't know what to say. Few understood the trainwreck unfolding in my heart. Amidst the relentless demands and isolating challenges, it often felt like I was speaking a language no one else could understand—and most days, I didn't even have the vocabulary to ask for help or to identify what help looked like.

After four decades in the caregiving trenches, I not only understand the chaos within a caregiver's heart but I've learned to speak "fluent caregiver." This book is born from that journey. It's not about long chapters, elaborate discourses or delayed help—caregivers simply don't have time for that. Instead, it's a collection of bite-sized wisdom gathered from years of experience.

These pages blend Scriptures that have strengthened me and served as the foundation of my faith, alongside hymns that lift my eyes, strengthen my spirit, and soothe my soul.

Each quote, Scripture, and hymn included here is more than a comforting phrase—they are lifelines in the storm, reminders that even in our most overwhelming moments, we are seen and held. This book invites fellow caregivers to pause, even if just for a moment, to find a sliver of peace, encouragement, and a sense of connection to the One who truly understands. I speak "fluent caregiver," but I've discovered it's our Savior's native tongue.

After each entry, you'll find space to jot down how it applies to your life today as a caregiver. Take the time to engage with these thoughts and when you revisit these pages in a few months, you'll notice growth, change, and, most importantly, God's strengthening presence in your journey.

May these words be more than just a companion on your path. Let them remind you that even when the road is steep and the nights are long, you are part of a greater story—one of resilience, faith, and an unyielding love holding us—particularly in those heartbreaking moments. He promises grace to meet us exactly where we are—whether in the laundry room, the hospital, the rehab center, the hospice or standing beside a grave. And through it all, may you find the strength to endure, the peace surpassing all understanding, and the hope lighting the way forward.

"Come to me, all who labor and are heavy laden,
and I will give you rest. Take my yoke upon you,
and learn from me, for I am gentle and lowly in heart,
and you will find rest for your souls.
For my yoke is easy, and my burden is light."

—Jesus, MATTHEW 11:28-30

"Grace"

is a beautiful word

for caregivers to remember.

To me, "Grace" is the loveliest name

in the English language—

I married a woman named Grace.

I love saying her name.

Grace, Grace, God's Grace.

Grace that will pardon and cleanse within;

Grace, Grace, God's Grace

Grace that is greater than all my sin.

—JULIA H. JOHNSTON,

"GRACE GREATER THAN OUR SIN"

My thoughts here ...

As caregivers, we often must make unilateral decisions that benefit the whole unit—not just one person. But we don't have to make those decisions in a vacuum.

Without counsel plans fail, but
with many advisers they succeed.
—PROVERBS 15:22

My thoughts here ...

WE FALL ASLEEP.
SLEEP CREEPS UP ON US.
BUT RESTING IS
A DECISION.

Jesus, I am resting, resting,
In the joy of what Thou art;
I am finding out the greatness
Of Thy loving heart.

— Jean Sophia Pigott,
"Jesus I Am Resting, Resting"

My thoughts here ...

Bringing meals is great for a short season but eventually someone needs to learn to buy groceries, plan meals, and cook—while also making a living. Helping someone acquire life skills as they serve as a caregiver equips them to endure and even thrive while caregiving.

But let each one test his own work,
and then his reason to boast will be in
himself alone and not in his neighbor.
For each will have to bear his own load.

—Galatians 6:4-5

My thoughts here ...

Caregivers require regular breaks, preferably without being criticized by others.

So then, there remains a Sabbath
rest for the people of God.
—HEBREWS 4:9

My thoughts here ...

The one we care for won't be helped by depleting ourselves emotionally, physically, and financially.

Blessed is the man who trusts in the Lord, whose trust is the Lord. He is like a tree planted by water, that sends out its roots by the stream, and does not fear when heat comes, for its leaves remain green, and is not anxious in the year of drought, for it does not cease to bear fruit.

—Jeremiah 17:7-8

My thoughts here ...

Healthy Caregivers Make Better Caregivers™

*Whoever brings blessing will
be enriched, and one who waters
will himself be watered.*

—Proverbs 11:25 ESV

My thoughts here ...

I developed a policy about people who criticize how I handle caregiving issues and the decisions I make as a caregiver: The length of time I will listen to someone criticize me is in direct proportion to how much time the critic spent helping.

Who are you to judge the servant of another? To his own master he stands or falls; and he will stand, for the Lord is able to make him stand.

—ROMANS 14:4

My thoughts here ...

If you love someone, you'll probably be a caregiver.

If you live long enough, you'll need one.

Even to your old age I am he,
and to gray hairs I will carry you.
I have made, and I will bear;
I will carry and will save.
—Isaiah 46:4

My thoughts here ...

Breathe.

Four seconds in;
Eight seconds out.

Breathe on me, Breath of God,
Fill me with life anew,
That I may love what Thou dost love,
And do what Thou wouldst do.

—EDWIN HATCH

My thoughts here ...

As a caregiver,
I'm no good to my wife
if I am fat, broke,
and miserable.

Awake, my soul, and with the sun
thy daily stage of duty run;
shake off dull sloth, and early rise
to pay thy morning sacrifice

—Thomas Ken,
"Awake my Soul and with the Sun"

My thoughts here ...

YOU CAN'T PUSH A WHEELCHAIR WITH CLENCHED FISTS.

See to it that no one fails to obtain the grace of God; that no "root of bitterness" springs up and causes trouble, and by it many become defiled.

—Hebrews 12:15

My thoughts here ...

Do the next right thing, and the next right thing may be to have a bowl of soup or take a nap.

And the angel of the Lord *came again a second time and touched him and said, "Arise and eat, for the journey is too great for you."*

—1 Kings 19:7

My thoughts here ...

I go back to Jesus's own words.

He said, I've come to give you life and life more abundantly.

Now, do I have to wait until we are in heaven and Gracie's body is restored and perfect and there's no more suffering and I'm not a caregiver anymore before I have an abundant life?

It's a good question, isn't it?

Must I have all the accouterments of fame and fortune in this life in order to live an abundant life?

That's also a good question.

But the Gospel is we have Christ.

We have Christ in a hospital room.

We have Christ in rehab.

We have Christ in divorce court.

We have Christ in a prison

We have Christ in a funeral home.

We have Christ no matter where we are, no matter what we're doing, no matter what is going on in our life,

If we have Christ, we have abundant life.

I came that they may have life

and have it abundantly.

—John 10:10

My thoughts here ...

Take Time for Stillness or Make Time for Illness

Be still, my soul; the Lord is on thy side;
bear patiently the cross of grief or pain.
Leave to thy God to order and provide;
in every change He faithful will remain.
Be still, my soul; thy best, thy heav'nly Friend
Through thorny ways leads to a joyful end."

—KATHRINA VON SCHLEGEL, "BE STILL MY SOUL"

My thoughts here ...

Be Well.

Be Safe.

Behave.

Training us to renounce ungodliness and worldly passions, and to live self-controlled, upright, and godly lives in the present age.

—Titus 2:12

My thoughts here ...

When I've struggled with demanding to know why God allows such difficult things, my father often quietly replied, "God's got this problem—He thinks HE'S God."

Be still, and know that I am God.
I will be exalted among the nations,
I will be exalted in the earth!
—Psalm 46:10

My thoughts here ...

Sin is a bigger problem than we think it is and the Cross is greater than we can imagine.

By canceling the record of debt that
stood against us with its legal demands.
This he set aside, nailing it to the cross.
—Colossians 2:14

My thoughts here ...

I've never had to make amends for something I didn't say, but I've sure had to make amends for things I did say.

When words are many,
transgression is not lacking,
but whoever restrains his lips is prudent.
—Proverbs 10:19

My thoughts here ...

When you feel like you have no idea
where you're going, slow down.
Don't try to look too far ahead,
and instead just do the next right thing.
Go back to what Scripture says,
"Thy word is a lamp unto my feet.'

It's a lamp—not a searchlight.

He drew me up from the pit of destruction,
out of the miry bog, and set my feet upon a rock,
making my steps secure.

—Psalm 40:2

My thoughts here ...

ASSURE RATHER THAN ARGUE.

A soft answer turns away wrath
but a harsh word stirs up anger.
—Proverbs 15:1

My thoughts here ...

Being right Is a poor substitute for being there.

And they sat with him on the ground seven days and seven nights, and no one spoke a word to him, for they saw that his suffering was very great.

—Job 2:13

My thoughts here ...

The human condition eventually leads us into places of fear and confusion where we all desperately need assurance—despite our abilities or inabilities. Ironically, we often discover more assurance for ourselves by offering it to others in distress.

Out in the highways and byways of life,
Many are weary and sad;
Carry the sunshine where darkness is rife,
Making the sorrowing glad.
—Ira B. Wilson, "Make Me A Blessing"

My thoughts here ...

Sometimes the greatest gift we can give to others struggling with heartbreaking decisions is to clear the room, quieten the noise, and sit with them.

We share our mutual woes,
our mutual burdens bear;
and often for each other flows
the sympathizing tears.
—John Fawcett, "Blest Be The Tie"

My thoughts here ...

While God's explanations of His actions are rare, His presence is constant.

And he said,

"My presence will go with you,

and I will give you rest."

—Exodus 33:14

My thoughts here ...

Sometimes you have to bite your tongue and learn to like the taste of blood.

Whoever guards his mouth and his tongue
guards his soul from trouble.
—Proverbs 21:23 (NASB)

My thoughts here ...

THE GOAL CANNOT BE TO FEEL BETTER. THE GOAL IS TO BE BETTER.

Teach me thy patience; still with thee
In closer, dearer company,
In work that keeps faith sweet and strong,
In trust that triumphs over wrong.

—Washington Gladden,
"O Master Let Me Walk With Thee"

My thoughts here ...

Friends Don't Let Friends "Caregive" Alone!

A friend loves at all times,
and a brother is born for adversity.
—PROVERBS 17:17

My thoughts here ...

It's okay to have stock answers for those on the periphery—not every one can be trusted with your pain and heartache.

It is better to take refuge in the Lord
than to trust in man.

—Psalm 118:8

My thoughts here ...

Most pastors would agree their theology is reflected in sermons, Sunday School lessons, small groups, hospital or home visits, and funeral services. But our theology also manifests with every toilet we clean, adult diaper we change, meal we serve (by hand as we help them eat), and each time we seek forgiveness for losing our cool.

We display our faith and doctrine when we humble ourselves to serve.

When he had washed their feet and put on his outer garments and resumed his place, he said to them, "Do you understand what I have done to you? You call me Teacher and Lord, and you are right, for so I am. If I then, your Lord and Teacher, have washed your feet, you also ought to wash one another's feet."—JOHN 13:12-14

My thoughts here ...

God uses many things in our lives to bring opportunities for sanctification to the forefront. And caregiving is a common (and effective) one. Caring for a chronically impaired loved one serves to illuminate character defects and theological weaknesses. In short, prolonged caregiving provides a front-row seat to the human condition.

For it is God who works in you,
both to will and to work for
his good pleasure.
—PHILIPPIANS 2:13

My thoughts here ...

Hospital rooms have a way of prompting honest reflections about how we feel about ourselves, one another, and God. Caring for a declining loved one forces internal conversations that rarely come any other way.

It is good for me that I was afflicted,
that I might learn your statutes.
—Psalm 119:71

My thoughts here ...

The "prosperity gospel" promulgated by all too many in evangelical circles comes up painfully short when faced with the reality of suffering, aging, and death. The human condition often serves as a wake-up call for bad doctrine.

So that we may no longer be children,
tossed to and fro by the waves and carried
about by every wind of doctrine, by human
cunning, by craftiness in deceitful schemes.

—EPHESIANS 4:14

My thoughts here ...

We minister from our wounds, for that is where we meet the Healer.

But he said to me, "My grace is sufficient for you, for my power is perfected in weakness." Therefore, I will most gladly boast all the more about my weaknesses, so that Christ's power may reside in me. So I take pleasure in weaknesses, insults, hardships, persecutions, and in difficulties, for the sake of Christ. For when I am weak, then I am strong.—2 CORINITHINIANS 12:9

My thoughts here ...

While many caregivers struggle with weight, the greatest weight is around our heart. Dealing appropriately with the weight carried by our heart better equips us to address our waistline.

Anxiety in a man's heart weighs him down,
but a good word makes him glad.
—PROVERBS 12:25

My thoughts here ...

You don't get a free pass to be an ass.

See that no one repays anyone evil for evil, but always seek to do good to one another and to everyone.—1 THESS. 5:15

My thoughts here ...

One can only wait for a rescue for so long before realizing a life must be lived—even in dire circumstances.

When thro' fiery trials thy pathway shall lie,
my grace, sufficient, shall be thy supply.
The flame shall not hurt thee; I only design,
Thy dross to consume and thy gold to refine.
—John Rippon, "How Firm a Foundation"

My thoughts here ...

Don't feel the need to correct people who consider themselves "instant experts" on the suffering our loved one endures. They don't know better; it's their problem, not ours.

If, however, your pastor is the one making you feel uncomfortable, find another church.

Leave the presence of a fool, for there you do not meet words of knowledge.

—PROVERBS 14:7

My thoughts here ...

You're not obligated to listen to others speculate about you or your loved one's condition. That applies doubly when self-promoters or their acolytes couch their speculation in "God- Talk."

Beloved, do not believe every spirit,
but test the spirits to see whether they are from God,
for many false prophets have gone out into the world.

—1 JOHN 4:1

My thoughts here …

We can walk away, even while pushing our loved one's wheelchair, without the need to correct others who criticize or treat us condescendingly with uniformed opinions. Better still, we can do that without feeling guilty—and without feeling rejected by God.

Guide me, O Thou great Jehovah,

Pilgrim through this barren land;

I am weak, but Thou art mighty;

Hold me with Thy powerful hand.

– William Williams,

"Guide Me, O Thou Great Jehovah"

(from the Welsh hymn, "Arglwydd, arwain trwy'r anialwch" which translates "Lord, Lead Me Through The Wilderness.")

My thoughts here ...

Faith healers don't spend time volunteering at the hospital for the same reason psychics don't win the lottery.

For such men are false apostles, deceitful workmen, disguising themselves as apostles of Christ. And no wonder, for even Satan disguises himself as an angel of light. So it is no surprise if his servants, also, disguise themselves as servants of righteousness. Their end will correspond to their deeds.—2 CORINTHIANS 11:13-15

My thoughts here ...

Resentment can lead even the best of hearts into poor judgment, malice, and even self-destruction. While life provides ample opportunities to hold a grudge, the resistance to do so remains a triumph of the human soul.

Let all bitterness and wrath and anger
and clamor and slander be put away from you,
along with all malice.

—Ephesians 4:31

My thoughts here ...

Be careful of financial planners who teach end-times prophecy on the side.

But concerning that day and hour
no one knows, not even the angels of heaven,
nor the Son, but the Father only.

—MATTHEW 24:36

My thoughts here ...

We cannot handle the weight of tending to the chronically ill by ourselves.

Nor does God expect us to do so.

When other helpers fail, and comforts flee,
Help of the helpless, O abide with me.
—Henry Lyte, "Abide With Me"

My thoughts here ...

Your source of love, your source of energy for all this has to come from someone other than yourself or your loved one—and the only person to go to is Christ.

Come, ye weary, heavy laden,
lost and ruined by the fall.
If you tarry till you're better,
you will never come at all.

—Joseph Hart,
"Come, Ye Sinners, Poor and Needy"

My thoughts here ...

The lottery is a tax on people who are bad at math.

Thinking peace comes when all is going our way serves as an emotional tax on people with poor understanding of the human condition.

And he told them a parable, saying, "The land of a rich man produced plentifully, and he thought to himself, 'What shall I do, for I have nowhere to store my crops?' And he said, 'I will do this: I will tear down my barns and build larger ones, and there I will store all my grain and my goods. And I will say to my soul, "Soul, you have ample goods laid up for many years; relax, eat, drink, be merry."' But God said to him, "Fool! This night your soul is required of you, and the things you have prepared, whose will they be?" So is the one who lays up treasure for himself and is not rich toward God. —LUKE 12:16-21

My thoughts here ...

Scripture teaches contentment rests in trusting God's provision in our uncertainties. No surgery, rehab program or bank account can take away the heartache of trauma, addiction, dementia or other impairments. Yet, trusting God with those and other challenges—however painful—provides us with the "currency of contentment" that allows us to be at peace amid our challenges.

When peace, like a river, attendeth my way
When sorrows like sea billows roll;
Whatever my lot, Thou hast taught me to say
It is well, it is well with my soul.

—Horatio Spafford,
"It Is Well With My Soul"

My thoughts here ...

Part of "...being better" is to offload the stress, heartbreak, and pain with a sense of humor. The tears flowing down our cheeks often dry with the smile of a lighter heart.

A joyful heart is good medicine,
but a crushed spirit dries up the bones.
—Proverbs 17:22

My thoughts here ...

If you have a carpet cleaner on retainer, you might be a caregiver.

And Sarah said, "God has made laughter for me; everyone who hears will laugh over me."

—Genesis 21:6

My thoughts here ...

Once while getting a manicure, the non-attentive manicurist blurted to my wife, "You're a pretty lady, you should get a pedicure."

Gracie, who has both legs amputated below the knee, replied, "But I don't have any feet!"

Without missing a beat, the busy manicurist replied, "Okay. Maybe next time."

...a time to weep, and a time to laugh.

—Ecclesiastes 3:4

My thoughts here ...

When learning complex medical tasks at home, it's okay to be confused—but it's not okay to be too embarrassed to ask for clarification.

Listen to advice and accept instruction,
that you may gain wisdom in the future.
—Proverbs 19:20

My thoughts here ...

While we can't guarantee it, our goal as caregivers is to one day stand at a grave. The question is, will we be standing there with clenched fists?

Will we resent our loved one, friends, and family who didn't help like we thought they should, others who may have caused or contributed to this condition?

Will we resent ourselves?

Will we resent God?

Or will we learn to live peacefully with ourselves, others, and God?

If possible, so far as it depends on you,

live peacefully with all.

—ROMANS 12:18

My thoughts here ...

My wife loves snow
and living in Montana, we see plenty.
But she reminds me after each snowfall
how it's a beautiful picture of God's grace
pristinely covering even the
most unseemly things.

Come now, let us reason together, says the LORD: though your sins are like scarlet, they shall be as white as snow; though they are red like crimson, they shall become like wool.

— Isaiah 1:18

My thoughts here ...

The only thing holding you back, truly, is you; not your loved ones' circumstances. Your mind is free. You are free to be as miserable or as joyful as you wish to be.

Count it all joy, my brothers, when you meet trials of various kinds, for you know that the testing of your faith produces steadfastness. And let steadfastness have its full effect, that you may be perfect and complete, lacking in nothing.—JAMES 1:2-4

My thoughts here ...

My wife has a Savior.

I'm not that Savior.

For there is one God, and there is one mediator
between God and men, the man Christ Jesus,
who gave himself as a ransom for all,
which is the testimony given at the proper time.

—1 TIMOTHY 2:5-6

My thoughts here ...

Thinking about your loved one's condition, look down at your hands. If you don't see nail prints, then this isn't yours to fix.

And my God will supply every need of yours according to his riches in glory in Christ Jesus.

—PHILLIPIANS 4:19

My thoughts here …

Wedding vows address long term care but not long term care facilities.

When I am sad at heart, teach me Thy way!
When earthly joys depart, Teach me Thy Way!
In hours of loneliness, in times of dire distress,
in failure or success, teach me Thy way.

—B. Mansell, Ramsey, "Teach Me Thy Way"

My thoughts here ...

Thus says the Lord *of hosts, the God of Israel, to all the exiles whom I have sent into exile from Jerusalem to Babylon: Build houses and live in them; plant gardens and eat their produce. Take wives and have sons and daughters; take wives for your sons, and give your daughters in marriage, that they may bear sons and daughters; multiply there, and do not decrease. But seek the welfare of the city where I have sent you into exile, and pray to the* Lord *on its behalf, for in its welfare you will find your welfare. For thus says the Lord of hosts, the God of Israel: Do not let your prophets and your diviners who are among you deceive you, and do not listen to the dreams that they dream, for it is a lie that they are prophesying to you in my name; I did not send them, declares the* Lord.

For thus says the Lord*: "When seventy years are completed for Babylon, I will visit you, and I will fulfill to you my promise and bring you back to this place. For I know the plans I have for you, declares the* Lord, *plans for welfare and not for evil, to give you a future and a hope.*

—Jeremiah 29:4-11

"Hope for the Caregiver"
is the conviction we as caregivers can live
a calmer, healthier, and—dare I say it?—a
more joyful life while serving as a caregiver.

My thoughts here ...

Caregivers need an annual physical and then six months later, a checkup for labs, blood pressure, etc. Why wait a whole year to discover high blood pressure, elevated sugar count or other easily detected warning signs?

Beloved, I pray that all may go well with you
and that you may be in good health,
as it goes well with your soul.

—3 JOHN 1:2

My thoughts here ...

There are sixty-five-plus million caregivers attending to the sickest in our country and statistics show that 72 percent of us fail to see our own physician regularly.

Do the math and "Houston—we have a problem!"

Or do you not know that your body is a temple
of the Holy Spirit within you, whom you have from God?
You are not your own, for you were bought with a price.
So glorify God in your body.

—1 CORINTHIANS 6:19-20

My thoughts here ...

What does it feel like to be a caregiver?

It's kind of like coming to a road, looking both ways—and then getting hit by a plane!

When the unexpected occurs (and it will), our stability must reside outside of our own abilities.

My hope is built on nothing less
Than Jesus' blood and righteousness;
I dare not trust the sweetest frame,
But wholly lean on Jesus' name.
On Christ, the solid Rock, I stand;
All other ground is sinking sand,
All other ground is sinking sand.

—EDWARD MOTE, "MY HOPE IS BUILT ON NOTHING LESS"

My thoughts here ...

Despite all our skills, blinding speed, and apparent competency, all caregivers suffer from the same challenge: what we do is unsustainable. It's simply a matter of time before a caregiver's body, emotions, and/or wallet breaks down.

We need a greater source of strength than our own.

My flesh and my heart may fail,
but God is the strength of my heart
and my portion forever.
—Psalm 73:26

My thoughts here ...

When caregivers recklessly hurl themselves at managing "that which cannot be managed," we rely on two things: our own abilities and the belief we will outlive our loved ones.

Both beliefs create a serious risk of harming the very people we seek to serve. If the caregiver goes down, this has disastrous implications for the loved one who is already vulnerable.

Wisdom dictates another path.

Every prudent man acts with knowledge,
but a fool flaunts his folly.
—PROVERBS 13:16

My thoughts here ...

While the end of
the trail for us as caregivers is
uncertain, there is no doubt however,
our loved ones will suffer even worse
than they do now if we, as
caregivers, are not in a safe and
healthy place today.

Listen to advice and accept instruction,
that you may gain wisdom in the future.
—PROVERBS 19:20

My thoughts here ...

Caregiving can often feel like a full-contact sport, and is hard on the body, as well as the heart. Call your primary care physician and keep the appointment. Doing so ensures treatment of the one body standing between your vulnerable loved one and an even worse disaster—yours!

But if anyone does not provide for his relatives,
and especially for members of his household,
he has denied the faith and is worse than an unbeliever.

—1 TIMOTHY 5:8

My thoughts here ...

Isolation often occurs due to logistics. Sometimes, it is not possible or practical for the caregiver to transport the loved one outside the home. Other times, caregivers, embarrassed about the condition of their loved ones or wishing to protect their dignity, remove themselves from the public eye. There are many reasons for the isolation caregivers feel but the results are universally negative. Without positive human connections, everybody suffers. That's why it's important for caregivers to remain engaged in church, community, and other social networks.

Two are better than one, because they have a good reward for their toil. For if they fall, one will lift up his fellow. But woe to him who is alone when he falls and has not another to lift him up! —ECCLESIASTES 4:9-10

My thoughts here ...

When we become isolated, our own dark thoughts take us down—often quickly. To best fight that, we need to surround ourselves with healthy, positive individuals. Sometimes it is as simple as a Facebook group but that can only go so far. Regular phone conversations, regular face-to-face conversations, and when possible, group events, serve as the path toward pushing back against isolation.

Grant, Lord, that with thy direction,
"Love each other," we comply,
Aiming with unfeigned affection Thy love to exemplify
—Nicolaus L. von Zinzendorf,
"Christian Hearts, in Love United"

My thoughts here ...

Serving as a caregiver is simply too difficult to do alone. Don't lean on your understanding, ask for guidance and help.

Don't believe everything you think!

The way of a fool is right in his own eyes,
But a wise man is he who listens to counsel.
—PROVERBS 12:15

My thoughts here ...

From personal safety to medical expertise, caregivers easily find themselves outmatched by an affliction and overpowered by fear.

What do you do with the fear?

I sought the Lord, and he answered me
and delivered me from all my fears.
—Psalm 34:4

My thoughts here ...

Stress leads many to want to eat more, yet if we choose to participate in healthy activities that calm us down, it will lesson our desire to graze. Once we're in a calmer frame of mind, we can tackle pushing ourselves a bit to exercise more and participate in healthier activities.

And put a knife to your throat
if you are given to appetite.
—Proverbs 23:2

My thoughts here ...

When a caregiver answers direct questions in third person singular (he, she, etc.) or first-person plural (we, our, us), it's a good indicator the loved one overshadows the caregiver's identity. When asked about our own hearts, however, we find ourselves caught off guard and usually struggle to share our feelings. This is why it is imperative for caregivers to find a trusted individual to whom they can speak in first person singular.

Jesus Loves ME

This I know.

For the Bible tells ME so.

—Anna Warner, "Jesus Loves Me"

My thoughts here ...

If life was a song, caregivers would struggle to sing the melody. Growing accustomed to someone else's voice, we find ourselves harmonizing; playing a supporting role. We avoid this by acknowledging our feelings out loud to a pastor, counselor, or trusted friend. Using our own voices, we can express, "I'm tired," "I'm lonely," "I'm scared," "I'm angry" or "I'm weary," and then seek (and receive) the help we need.

I must tell Jesus all of my trials;
I cannot bear these burdens alone;
In my distress He kindly will help me;
He ever loves and cares for His own.
—Elisha Hoffman, "I Must Tell Jesus"

My thoughts here ...

Caregivers often feel lonely in a crowded room—and on a crowded pew.

So she called the name of the Lord who spoke to her,
"You are a God of seeing," for she said,
"Truly here I have seen him who looks after me."
—Genesis 16:13

My thoughts here ...

When a trusted friend asks how you are doing, it may feel strange at first but try and answer in first person singular and remember, appropriately sharing your ownheartache and feelings is not self-centered; it is healthy.

And though a man might prevail
against one who is alone, two will withstand him
—a threefold cord is not quickly broken.

—ECCLESIASTES 4:12

My thoughts here ...

While bravery and action remains important, discretionary valor is equally, if not more, essential as a caregiver. That discretion of knowing when to act, speak or be still—comes with time and practice but remains an important part of our journey in becoming healthy caregivers.

Discretion will watch over you,
understanding will guard you.
—PROVERBS 2:11

My thoughts here ...

As caregivers, we sadly (and harshly) judge ourselves on our performance while completely overlooking our attendance record—which is flawless.

And let us not grow weary of doing good,
for in due season we will reap, if we do not give up.
—Galatians 6:9

My thoughts here ...

We're no good to anyone if we allow the stress of guilt to push us to the brink of emotional or physical collapse.

There's a better way to deal with any guilt we carry.

If we confess our sins,
he is faithful and just to forgive us our sins
and to cleanse us from all unrighteousness.

—1 John 1:9

My thoughts here ...

I know there will be sorrow,
we'll face that somehow.
But my hands can't hold tomorrow;
I can only hold you now.

—"I Can Only Hold You Now," words and music by Peter Rosenberger and Buddy Mondlock ©Gray Park Media, LLC and Fire & Change Music

Therefore do not be anxious about tomorrow,
for tomorrow will be anxious for itself.
Sufficient for the day is its own trouble.
—MATTHEW 6:34

My thoughts here ...

We become gracious when extending to others the same grace we desire for ourselves.

Be kind to one another,
tenderhearted, forgiving one another,
as God in Christ forgave you.
—EPHESIANS 4:32

My thoughts here …

When recovery is unattainable, the journey of discovery beckons.

I came to Jesus as I was,
Weary, worn, and sad;
I found in Him a resting-place,
And He has made me glad.

—Horatius Bonar, "I Heard the Voice of Jesus Say"

My thoughts here ...

We often deny what our eyes clearly see because it's painful to admit what's happening.

But truth is truth.

Truth is not ours or someone else's—truth is reality.

And you will know the truth,

and the truth will set you free.

—John 8:32

My thoughts here ...

Don't stumble on something behind you.

Let your eyes look directly forward,
and your gaze be straight before you.
Ponder the path of your feet;
then all your ways will be sure.

—PROVERBS 4:25-26

My thoughts here ...

While many yearn for the "big victories," sometimes the win for caregivers can be a less painful walk through the often drama-filled caregiving journey.

Better is a dry morsel with quiet
than a house full of feasting with strife.
—Proverbs 17:1

My thoughts here ...

If we refuse to accept the reality of what we're facing, we'll never fully grasp or respect the magnitude of the challenges before us. Growth begins with acceptance.

Just as I am, though tossed about
With many a conflict, many a doubt,
Fightings within, and fears without,
O Lamb of God, I come, I come.

—Charlotte Elliott, "Just As I Am"

My thoughts here ...

When weary,
sometimes it's best
to hold your tongue,
enjoy a private laugh,
and maybe even have
a quiet meal.

A fool gives full vent to his spirit,
but a wise man quietly holds it back.
—PROVERBS 29:11

My thoughts here ...

Caregiving breeds isolation and isolation distorts perception—which leads to significant challenges. Asking for clairification, regardless of embarrassments, always trumps misunderstanding.

The beginning of wisdom is this:
Get wisdom, and whatever you get, get insight.
—PROVERBS 4:7

My thoughts here ...

Some things won't be fixed on this side of Heaven and they are too big for me to carry. So, mentally (and spiritually), I put those in a "box of things God will have to redeem." I don't demand He change those things; rather, I accept He alone has the power to do so.

He will wipe away every tear from their eyes,
and death shall be no more, neither shall there be
mourning, nor crying, nor pain anymore,
for the former things have passed away."

—Revelation 21:4

My thoughts here ...

After decades of trying to carry the impossible, I find I breathe easier and live more peacefully when trusting God with all the broken pieces. Remembering Jesus was a carpernter further bolsters my faith—knowing He doesn't even waste the sawdust.

Be still, my soul; thy Jesus can repay
from His own fullness all He takes away.
—Kathrina von Schlegel, "Be Still My Soul"

My thoughts here ...

We fight
until the end—
not to avoid death
but to fully
embrace life.

I will praise the Lord as long as I live;
I will sing praises to my God while I have my being.

—PSALM 146:2

My thoughts here ...

Victories, however tiny, define our progress.

A slack hand causes poverty,
but the hand of the diligent makes rich.
—PROVERBS 10:4

My thoughts here ...

Like the first steps my wife took on prosthetic limbs, each positive step we take with our wounded souls is a victory.

Through many dangers, toils, and snares,
I have already come;
'Tis grace hath brought me safe thus far,
And grace will lead me home.
—JOHN NEWTON, "AMAZING GRACE"

My thoughts here ...

Our responsibility as caregivers is to see the bigger picture when our loved ones can't.

With upright heart he shepherded them
and guided them with his skillful hand.

—Psalm 78:72

My thoughts here ...

As caregivers,
we owe it to ourselves
to inventory the people
around us who have
access to our hearts.

But test everything;
hold fast what is good.
—1 Thessalonians 5:21

My thoughts here ...

Once caregivers speak in their own voice—in first person singular—a real conversation can occur and the path to healthiness begins.

Take my voice, and let me sing
Always, only, for my King;
Take my lips, and let them be
Filled with messages from Thee.

—Frances Havergal, "Take My Life and Let It Be"

My thoughts here ...

When asked how they are doing, many caregivers can recite their loved one's chart. But the path to healthiness is speaking from our own hearts—sharing about what's going on with us.

Come and hear, all you who fear God,
and I will tell what he has done for my soul.
I cried to him with my mouth,
and high praise was on my tongue.
—PSALM 66:16-17

My thoughts here ...

An often overlooked "identity theft" is the one that affects family caregivers—we struggle to speak in our own voice.

But now thus says the Lord, he who created you,
O Jacob, he who formed you, O Israel:
"Fear not, for I have redeemed you;
I have called you by name, you are mine."

—Isaiah 43:1

My thoughts here ...

We may not know the science about our loved one's condition, but we know them. That knowledge and experience form what I call "Caregiver Authority," and it's imperitive we bring that to any discssion on the plan of care for our loved ones.

I know that the Lord will maintain
the cause of the afflicted,
and will execute justice for the needy.
—Psalm 140:12

My thoughts here ...

THE BEST COUNSEL REGARDING ONE'S CAREGIVING JOURNEY COMES FROM THOSE WITH CREDIBLE EXPERIENCE.

Whoever walks with the wise becomes wise,

but the companion of fools will suffer harm.

—Proverbs 13:20

My thoughts here ...

Resentment gnaws at our souls. As caregivers, we already bear enough. Lose the grudges— but keep the boundaries.

Let all bitterness and wrath and anger
and clamor and slander be put away from you,
along with all malice.

—Ephesians 4:31

My thoughts here ...

Even if their poor behavior results in unpleasant consequences for our loved ones (and often us), we are not required to be miserable while caring for them.

When upon life's billows you are tempest-tossed,
When you are discouraged, thinking all is lost,
Count your many blessings, name them one by one,
And it will surprise you what the Lord has done.
—Johnson Oatman, "Count Your Blessings"

My thoughts here ...

The scriptures tell us to "honor our mother and father..." not honor addiction or alcoholism or abuse. One can honor them, while keeping healthy boundaries.

Honor your father and your mother,
that your days may be long in the land
that the Lord your God is giving you.

—Exodus 20:12

My thoughts here ...

While action and planning remain essential, we better serve ourselves (and our loved ones) by the discretion of knowing when to act, speak or be still. In doing so, we can give ourselves a medal for "discretionary valor."

Set a guard, O Lord, over my mouth;
keep watch over the door of my lips!
—Psalm 141:3

My thoughts here ...

Our scared hands are held by His scarred hand.

Behold, I have engraved you
on the palms of my hands....

—ISAIAH 49:16

My thoughts here ...

As believers, we are all called to minister to those who are sick, outcast, hungry, thirsty, and imprisoned—our Savior remains clear about that directive. Sometimes, it's simply sitting silently with those in grief. Doing so often provides the opportunity to agonize, to groan, to mourn.

Is not this the fast that I choose: to loose the bonds of wickedness, to undo the straps of the yoke, to let the oppressed go free, and to break every yoke? Is it not to share your bread with the hungry and bring the homeless poor into your house; when you see the naked, to cover him, and not to hide yourself from your own flesh?

—Isaiah 58:6-7

My thoughts here ...

The grief-stricken have their own timetable and we respect their trauma by providing company more than words—companionship through the often-long valley of the shadow of death.

Be near me, still, O God,
When tempests fierce arise;
And when the storms of trouble roll,
Hide Thou my soul.

—UNKNOWN

My thoughts here ...

When raging, despairing, or "putting on a good face," we fail to mourn—and remain without comfort. Mourning involves accepting what is and grieving over the brokenness. Furthermore, grieving takes as long as it takes, and it cannot be coerced. We can sit with those who suffer and strengthen them with our presence but the sermons and well-worn phrases must wait at the door.

Blessed are those who mourn,

for they shall be comforted.

—Matthew 5:4

My thoughts here ...

Supporting someone in pain can be uncomfortable. Job's friends were initially silent but when they spoke up, they presented more than thirty chapters of poor theology, highlighting the futility of trying to understand God's ways.

People in trauma require comfort, not speculating about God's plans.

I will stand with you, when you cannot stand alone.
I will fight for you, when all your strength is gone.
I will sing for you, so all can hear your song.
Take my hand, lean on me, we will stand.

—"We Will Stand" words /music by Peter and Gracie Rosenberger @2003 Gray Park Media

My thoughts here ...

Painful circumstances require few words—there will be time for those later.

Silently now I wait for Thee,
Ready my God, Thy will to see,
Open my ears, illumine me,
Spirit divine!

—Clara Scott, "Open My Eyes, That I May See"

My thoughts here …

Respect

the trauma.

One man was there who had been
an invalid for thirty-eight years.
When Jesus saw him lying there and knew
that he had already been there a long time....

—John 5:6-7

My thoughts here ...

"Plate spinning" makes a great vaudeville act but it is not recommended as a permanent lifestyle for serving as a family caregiver. Diligence is better than frenetics.

The hand of the diligent will rule,
while the slothful will be put to forced labor.
—Proverbs 12:24

My thoughts here ...

Sometimes, you have to buy your own Valentine's Day or birthday card. It's not that they don't want to—they simply can't. On that occasion(s), buy one that speaks to your heart and celebrates you in a way that pierces your soul. If it's a Valentine's Day card, buy one that poignantly honors the love the two of you share.

If it's a birthday card, before mailing it to yourself, slip in a ten dollar bill—or a twenty if needed.

If there are tears on the card, that's okay. Your Heavenly Father sees—and celebrates with you.

So that your giving may be in secret.

And your Father who sees in secret will reward you.

—Matthew 6:4

My thoughts here ...

Some may question the value of hymns based on age but they miss the deeper essence that gives these timeless melodies their enduring power. Hymns are more than just songs; they embody rich truths—compact theology—intricately woven into the fabric of music.

When we sing them as we struggle, people listen.

About midnight Paul and Silas were
praying and singing hymns to God,
and the prisoners were listening to them.

—Acts 16:25

My thoughts here ...

When the heart hurts and words fail, we may feel lost. Yet, leafing through a hymnal allows us to see the words of those who understood those experiences and more. Through the centuries, hymns have offered words and tunes to strengthen our souls, reminding us we are never alone in our struggles. In these hymns, we find solace, hope, and a reminder of God's enduring love and grace.

Let the word of Christ dwell in you richly,
teaching and admonishing one another in all wisdom,
singing psalms and hymns and spiritual songs,
with thankfulness in your hearts to God.

—COLOSSIANS 3:16

My thoughts here ...

It's been said, expectations are embryonic resentments and for caregivers, letting go of those expectations remains a critical step to living more peacefully with a heartbreaking set of circumstances. Letting go will always come with sadness and not a few tears. Yet in those tears, God promises not only comfort, but life itself.

This is my comfort in my affliction,
that your promise gives me life.
—Psalm 119:50

My thoughts here ...

Caregiving is not an excuse to avoid living.

Therefore, since we are surrounded by so great a cloud of witnesses, let us also lay aside every weight, and sin which clings so closely, and let us run with endurance the race that is set before us, looking to Jesus, the founder and perfecter of our faith, who for the joy that was set before him endured the cross, despising the shame, and is seated at the right hand of the throne of God.—HEBREWS 12:1-2

My thoughts here ...

There is a point during the caregiving journey where we cease to emote about it and accept this as our life. It's a challenging life, but it doesn't have to be a bad one.

Have Thine own way, Lord, Have Thine own, way.
Thou art the potter, I am the clay..
Mold me and make me after Thy will.
While I am waitig. Yielded and still.

Have Thine own way, Lord, Have Thine own, way.
Hold o'er my being absolute sway.
Fill with Thy Spirit till all shall see
Christ only, always, living in me.

—Adelaide Pollard, "Have Thine Own Way"

My thoughts here ...

Time has a way of lessening pain to the point where you're not reacting like it happened just at that moment.

He has made everything beautiful in its time.
Also, he has put eternity into man's heart,
yet so that he cannot find out what God has done
from the beginning to the end.

—Ecclesiates 3:11

My thoughts here ...

Our circumstances do not get to dictate our joy.

Whatever my lot, Thou hast taught me to say,
It is well, it is well with my soul.
—HORATIO SPAFFORD. "IT IS WELL WITH MY SOUL"

My thoughts here …

You're stronger than you think you are but you don't have to be strong all the time.

He gives power to the faint, and to him who has no might he increases strength. Even youths shall faint and be weary, and young men shall fall exhausted; but they who wait for the Lord shall renew their strength; they shall mount up with wings like eagles; they shall run and not be weary; they shall walk and not faint.

—Isaiah 40:29-31

My thoughts here ...

It's okay to
not be okay
but it's not okay
to stay that way.

I remember my affliction and my wandering,
the bitterness and the gall. I well remember them,
and my soul is downcast within me.
Yet this I call to mind and therefore I have hope:
Because of the Lord's great love we are not consumed,
for his compassions never fail.
They are new every morning; great is your faithfulness.
I say to myself, The Lord is my portion;
therefore I will wait for him.

—LAMENTATIONS 3:19-24

My thoughts here ...

The most important thing you can do for your loved one is to take care of yourself first.

And he said to them,
"Come away by yourselves to a desolate place
and rest a while." For many were coming and going,
and they had no leisure even to eat.

—MARK 6:31

My thoughts here ...

Laughter offers release as well as a break from the stresses of what is often a very difficult season of life for both the caregiver and the one for whom care is given.

Then our mouth was filled with laughter,
and our tongue with shouts of joy;
then they said among the nations,
"The Lord has done great things for them.
The Lord has done great things for us;
we are glad."—PSALM 126:2

My thoughts here ...

If you're going to judge yourself by your performance record, then at least be fair and also factor in your attendance record—which is perfect, by the way.

Therefore, my beloved brothers,
be steadfast, immovable, always abounding
in the work of the Lord, knowing that in the Lord
your labor is not in vain.

—1 CORINTHIANS 15:58

My thoughts here ...

Our loved one's circumstances aren't holding us back. We do that to ourselves.

But Moses said to the Lord, "Oh, my Lord, I am not eloquent, either in the past or since you have spoken to your servant, but I am slow of speech and of tongue." Then the Lord said to him, "Who has made man's mouth? Who makes him mute, or deaf, or seeing, or blind? Is it not I, the Lord? Now therefore go, and I will be with your mouth and teach you what you shall speak." But he said, "Oh, my Lord, please send someone else." Then the anger of the Lord was kindled against Moses and he said, "Is there not Aaron, your brother, the Levite? I know that he can speak well. Behold, he is coming out to meet you, and when he sees you, he will be glad in his heart."

—Exodus 4:10-14

My thoughts here ...

Our minds can be a prison or a palace—it all depends upon what we choose to think about and meditate upon.

O Lord my God, when I in awesome wonder
consider all the works Thy hands have made.
I see the stars, I hear the mighty thunder,
Thy power throughout the universe displayed.
—Carl Boberg, "How Great Thou Art"

My thoughts here ...

As caregivers, acceptance connects our brains to our hearts and allows "what is" to mingle with grief. In the process, we can live more peacefully with the often chaotic events in our lives—and our resolve to do so can also help dry the more than occasional tears.

May I be willing, Lord, to bear
Daily my cross for Thee;
Even Thy cup of grief to share,
Thou hast borne all for me.
Lest I forget Gethsemane,
Lest I forget Thine agony;
Lest I forget Thy love for me,
Lead me to Calvary.

—JENNIE E. HUSSEY, "LEAD ME TO CALVARY"

My thoughts here ...

In trauma, the clock is the adversary but in caregiving, it's the calendar. While emergencies demand an immediate response, quick actions for caregivers often result in several battles on multiple fronts. Nothing stretches a caregiver too thin like rushing to a crisis while already embroiled in one.

My son, do not lose sight of these—keep sound wisdom and discretion, and they will be life for your soul and adornment for your neck. Then you will walk on your way securely, and your foot will not stumble."

—PROVERBS 3:21-23

My thoughts here ...

Being still often takes enormous discipline and is its own form of bravery. Although some may not recognize it, knowing when to act—or when not to—often reflects extraordinary wisdom and courage.

Drop Thy still dews of quietness,
Till all our strivings cease;
Take from our souls the strain and stress,
And let our ordered lives confess
The beauty of Thy peace.

—John Greenleaf Whittier,
"Dear Lord and Father Of Mankind"

My thoughts here ...

Although not often valued, discretionary valor remains one of the most critical attributes a caregiver can utilize. While soldiers receive medals reflecting bravery under duress, our medals for discretionary valor—the ability to not act or speak rashly—appear differently.

Our awards signify peace of mind, less drama, and a good night's sleep.

Whoever is wise, let him understand these things;
whoever is discerning, let him know them;
for the ways of the Lord are right,
and the upright walk in them,
but transgressors stumble in them.

—Hosea 14:9

My thoughts here ...

Our heavenly Father often doesn't give us the answers we demand. Yet, He does give us the assurance we need; the assurance of His presence and love for us—particularly in the midst of our struggles.

The Lord your God is in your midst,
a mighty one who will save;
he will rejoice over you with gladness;
he will quiet you by his love;
he will exult over you with loud singing.

—Zephaniah 3:17

My thoughts here ...

Serving as a caregiver is not a "sentence," punishment or an incarceration. We're tethered—not chained. While we may be stretched and challenged, with creativity and resourcefulness, we can live a full, passionate, and productive life—all while serving as a caregiver.

Because love has been lavished so upon me, Lord
A wealth I know that was not meant for me to hoard,
I shall give love to those in need,
shall show that love by word and deed:
Thus shall my thanks be thanks indeed.

—Noll Crowell, "Because I Have Been Given Much"

My thoughts here ...

RELATIONSHIPS ARE LIKE SHOES: THEY'RE NOT MUCH GOOD IF THEY DON'T FIT.

Do two walk together,

unless they have agreed to meet?

—AMOS 3:3

My thoughts here ...

Caregiving often feels likes hours of frustration and grief interrupted by moments of boredom.

Have you not known? Have you not heard?
The Lord is the everlasting God,
the Creator of the ends of the earth.
He does not faint or grow weary;
his understanding is unsearchable.

—Isaiah 40:28

My thoughts here ...

There are few things in life so bad that ice cream can't make better.

When David came to Mahanaim, Shobi the son of Nahash from Rabbah of the Ammonites, and Machir the son of Ammiel from Lo-debar, and Barzillai the Gileadite from Rogelim brought beds, basins, pottery, wheat, barley, flour, roasted grain, broad beans, lentils, and [other] roasted grain, honey, cream, sheep, and cheese of the herd, for David and the people who were with him, to eat; for they said, "The people are hungry and weary and thirsty in the wilderness."

—2 SAMUEL 17:27-29 (AMP)

My thoughts here ...

Anytime we set boundaries, we can expect pushback. The ones who don't like my boundaries are the ones who profit when I don't have them.

"A man without self-control
is like a city broken into
and left without walls."
—PROVERBS 25:28

My thoughts here ...

Desperate Times Call for Anchored Faith.

When darkness veils his lovely face,
I rest on his unchanging grace;
in every high and stormy gale,
my anchor holds within the veil.

—Edward Mote,
"My Hope Is Built On Nothing Less"

My thoughts here ...

I've tried for a lifetime to offer my consulting services to the Almighty. He's yet to take me up on it.

For my thoughts are not your thoughts,
neither are your ways my ways, declares the Lord.
For as the heavens are higher than the earth,
so are my ways higher than your ways
and my thoughts than your thoughts.

—Isaiah 55:8-9

My thoughts here ...

I've witnessed a curiosity in that the further people are distanced from affliction—their own or that of others—the weaker their theology becomes.

Before I was afflicted I went astray,

but now I keep your word.

—Psalm 119:67

My thoughts here ...

Peter Rosenberger has entered his fortieth year as a caregiver to his wife, Gracie—severely injured before they met. After their marriage, her medical challenges surged. Gracie has endured ninety-eight operations, including the amputation of both legs, lives with relentless chronic pain, and has been treated by more than 100 physicians across thirteen hospitals—with medical bills exceeding $20 million.

From this crucible, Peter emerged as the nation's leading voice for family caregivers. His nationally syndicated radio program, *Hope for the Caregiver*, is the largest of its kind—offering practical help, piercing clarity, contagious humor, and the hope of the Gospel to those carrying burdens too heavy to bear alone.

Peter's extensive list of published commentaries includes *Fox News, The Washington Times, AARP, Guideposts, Mature Living, Gannett, Tribune Media*, and more. He is the author of five books and the co-founder—alongside Gracie—of *Standing With Hope*, a nonprofit providing prosthetic limbs and caregiver support.

Peter and Gracie have two sons, Parker (and Viveka) and Grayson; five grandchildren; and live in the mountains of Southwest Montana—**where the sky's big, the altitude's high, and the coffee's strong.**

Learn more at PeterRosenberger.com

A
MINUTE
for
Caregivers
When Every Day Feels
Like Monday
PETER ROSENBERGER

Standing With Hope is the ministry founded by Gracie and Peter Rosenberger. The organization focuses on "the Wounded and Those Who Care for Them" through two programs: a prosthetic limb outreach for amputees and an outreach to family caregivers.

Peter and Gracie invite you to join their mission by visiting standingwithhope.com.

FOREWORD BY KEN TADA
Hope for the Caregiver
Encouraging Words to Strengthen Your Spirit
PETER ROSENBERGER
Foreword by Jeff Foxworthy
Gracie
standing with hope
GRACIE ROSENBERGER
as told to Peter W. Rosenberger
7 CARE GIVER LAND MINES
And How You Can Avoid Them
PETER W. ROSENBERGER
PETER ROSENBERGER
SONGS FOR THE
CAREGIVER
PETER ROSENBERGER
SONGS FOR THE
CAREGIVER
Gracie
Resilient